# DIY

# Homemade Hand Sanitizer and Homemade Face Mask

The Ultimate Guide to Make Your Own Hand Sanitizer and Reusable Cloth Face Mask in 10 Minutes or Less

(2 Books In 1)

By

Dr. Lee Henton

# Copyright © 2020 – Dr. Lee Henton

## All rights reserved

No part of this publication may be reproduced, distributed, or transmitted in any form or by any means, including photocopying, recording, or other electronic or mechanical methods, without the prior written permission of the publisher, except in the case of brief quotations embodied in reviews and certain other non-commercial uses permitted by copyright law.

## Disclaimer

This publication is designed to provide reliable information on the subject matter only for educational purposes, and it is not intended to provide medical advice for any medical treatment. You should always consult your doctor or physician for guidance before you stop, start, or alter any prescription medications or attempt to implement the methods discussed. This book is published independently by the author and has no affiliation with any brands or products mentioned within it. The author hereby disclaims any responsibility or liability whatsoever that is incurred from the use or application of the contents of this publication by the purchaser or reader. The purchaser or reader is hereby responsible for his or her own actions.

## This 2-In-1 Bundle Consists of Two Parts:

### Part I - The 5-Minutes DIY Homemade Hand Sanitizer

A Step by Step Guide on How to Use Natural Essential Oils to Make Your Own Hand Sanitizer Gel and Spray Recipes

### Part II - The 10-Minutes DIY Homemade Face Mask

A Step By Step Beginners Guide to Make Your Own Protective, Washable, and Reusable Cloth Face Mask With Illustrations Included

## Books By The Same Author

| No | Title |
|----|-------|
| 1 | The Secrets of Vagus Nerve Stimulation |
| **A Special Do-It-Yourself Homemade Guide to Protect You From Viruses and Bacteria** ||
| 2 | The 5-Minutes DIY Homemade Hand Sanitizer |
| 3 | The 10 Minutes DIY Homemade Face Mask |
| **Other Books Co-written By The Author** ||
| 4 | The Budget-Friendly Renal Diet Cookbook |

# Table of Contents

Books By The Same Author .................................................... 4

About The Author ................................................................ 10

PART I ................................................................................. 11

Introduction ........................................................................ 12

Chapter 1 ............................................................................ 16

The ABC of Hand Sanitizers ................................................. 16

    Hand Sanitizer and Its Importance ..................................... 17

    Hand Sanitizers Vs. Hand Washing ..................................... 18

    Alcohol-Based Sanitizers Vs. Alcohol-Free Sanitizers ...... 20

    Effectiveness of Hand Sanitizers Against Germs ............... 21

        What Germs Can Alcohol-Based Hand Sanitizer Kill? 22

    DIY Hand Sanitizer Benefits ................................................ 25

    Are DIY Hand Sanitizers Safe? ............................................ 28

Chapter 2 ............................................................................ 31

Making Homemade Sanitizers ............................................. 31

    Hand Sanitizer Tools You Need to Have ........................... 31

    Hand Sanitizer Ingredients You Need to Get ..................... 34

- Isopropyl (Rubbing Alcohol) or Ethanol .......................... 34
- Aloe Vera Gel .......................... 35
- Essential Oils .......................... 36
- Hand Sanitizer Ingredient You Must Not Use .......................... 37
  - Vodka .......................... 38
  - Witch Hazel .......................... 39
- Safety Precautions for Making Your Hand Sanitizers ...... 40
- Recipes For Homemade Hand Sanitizers .......................... 44
  - The WHO Hand Sanitizer Formula .......................... 44
  - Simple Standard Hand Sanitizer .......................... 46
  - Vitamin E Oil Hand Sanitizer .......................... 47
  - Kid-Friendly Hand Sanitizers By Age Group .......................... 48
- Citrus Mint Hand Sanitizer .......................... 49
- Lavender-Tea Tree "Little Tykes" Hand Sanitizer .......................... 50
- Thieves Hand Sanitizer .......................... 51
- Glycerin-Based Hand Sanitizer .......................... 52

Chapter 3 .......................... 54

Hand Hygiene Practice .......................... 54
- Why Is It important? .......................... 55
- Handwashing the Right Way .......................... 56

Using Hand Sanitizers Effectively ............................................. 58

Conclusion .................................................................................. 60

References .................................................................................. 62

PART II ....................................................................................... 65

Introduction ............................................................................... 66

Chapter 1 .................................................................................... 70

The ABC of Face Mask .............................................................. 70

   What is Face Mask ............................................................... 71

   Types of Face Mask and Recommendations For Usage ... 71

      N95 Respirator .................................................................. 72

      Medical (Surgical) Face Mask ......................................... 74

      Homemade Cloth Face Mask .......................................... 76

   Are Face Masks Effective Against Virus Infection? .......... 76

   Why You Should Make Your Own Face Mask .................. 81

   Reusing and Disposing of Face Mask ................................. 82

Chapter 2 .................................................................................... 88

DIY Homemade Face Mask ...................................................... 88

   Best Fabrics For Reusable Homemade Mask ..................... 88

   Are Fabric Face Masks Really Effective? ............................ 89

Are Coffee Filters, Paper Towels, and Tissues Effective? 90

Making Homemade Face Mask .................................................. 91

Sewing Method .......................................................................... 91

    List of Materials and Tools ................................................. 92

    Step 1: Measurement and Cut List ..................................... 92

    Step 2: Fold and Sew Along The Top Edge ..................... 94

    Step 3: Pin Elastic or Fabric Ties ........................................ 96

    Step 4: Sew The Sides To Secure The Elastic or Ties ..... 97

    Step 5: Insert a Metal Wire For Nose Cover ................... 98

    Step 6: Make The Pleats ...................................................... 98

    Step 7: Insert The Filter .................................................... 100

No-Sewing "Emergency" Method ......................................... 101

    List of Materials ................................................................. 101

    Step 1: Prepare Your Fabric ............................................. 102

    Step 2: Make The First and Second Folds ..................... 102

    Step 3: Fold The Ends of the Fabric ............................... 103

    Step 4: Insert The Rubber Bands .................................... 103

    Step 5: Lift The Mask to Your Face ................................ 104

Chapter 3 ..................................................................................... 106

Best Practice For Handling Face Mask ................................. 106

    Wearing Face Masks The Right Way ............................... 106

    Removing Face Masks The Right Way ............................ 109

Conclusion ............................................................................. 111

References ............................................................................. 113

## About The Author

Dr. Lee Henton is a US-trained General Practice Doctor from the Johns Hopkins University School of Medicine with additional qualification in nutritional medicine from Iowa State University. He is a certified specialist in dietology and nutrition.

He has extensive years of medical and nutritional experience across general medicine, pediatrics, traumatology, addictions, food nutrition, and diet therapy.

He currently runs a co-established private medical and wellness practice where he operates from. His approach is personalized with each client by combining medical and food nutrition counseling. All advice he provides is at par with his experience, as well as with medical and nutritional concepts. He specializes primarily in men and women's health.

He lives in Minnesota with his wife and two daughters.

# PART I

**The 5-Minutes DIY Homemade Hand Sanitizer**

A Step by Step Guide on How to Use Natural Essential Oils to Make Your Own Hand Sanitizer Gel and Spray Recipes

# Introduction

Since the outbreak of COVID-19, sales of hand sanitizers have soared tremendously, resulting in not only its scarcity but also the unnecessary increase in its cost of purchase virtually in most online stores, pharmacies, and supermarkets. This is exactly what happens when the demand exceeds the supply.

According to the World Health Organization (WHO) and U.S. Centers for Disease Control and Prevention (CDC), hand washing is by far the most effective way to not only destroy the coronavirus but also protect yourself from most bacteria and viruses, while recommending that hand sanitizers be used only when hand washing is practically unforeseeable. Hand sanitizers with an alcohol concentration of 60% and above are recognized by WHO and CDC as very effective in destroying most germs, which includes the coronavirus; however, not all commercially sold hand sanitizers are made effective against this virus, and most likely, against other bacteria and viruses because of the lower concentration of alcohol it contains. This has made homemade hand sanitizers much more appealing, where buying at an overpriced amount can finally be averted, but most importantly, where greater control over the ingredients and the quality of the hand sanitizer can be exercised. With that being said, making your own hand sanitizer is not a walk in the park, especially for an average consumer who knows nothing about the right ingredients to use, the safety precautions that must be adhered to, and the ratio of alcohol to ingredients that must be followed to produce the final 60% and above concentration. It could be a mess if you don't get this right. Not to worry, this book is designed to take you through each step of the process on the dos and don'ts of making your own hand sanitizer at home. And not just that, this book uses an easy to understand language with little to no scientific jargon, even if you don't have a background in science.

At the end of this book, you will:

- Gain a deeper understanding of how hand sanitizers work against bacteria and viruses such as coronavirus, its importance, and its dos and don'ts.

- Be enlightened on why alcohol-based hand sanitizers should be used over alcohol-free hand sanitizers.
- Know the type of germs alcohol-based hand sanitizers can destroy and what type it cannot destroy.
- Understand the real benefits of making your own hand sanitizer.
- Know why you must not use certain ingredients recommended over the internet to make your own hand sanitizer.
- Uncover all you need to get started in making your own hand sanitizer, thereby subtracting the noise and inconsistencies all over the internet.
- Be well educated on the important safety precautions you must adhere to when making your own hand sanitizer.
- Be familiar with the necessary tools, ingredients, and steps you need to follow to make your own WHO and CDC recommended hand sanitizer.

- Know how to prepare several homemade hand sanitizer recipes in 5 minutes, using the right alcohol proportion and different essential oil ingredients that are both safe for your kids, families, and friends and effective against most bacteria and viruses, e.g., coronavirus.
- Be better informed on when to wash your hands over when to use hand sanitizers against germs.
- Understand what hand hygiene entails, its importance and how to apply it correctly during hand washing and usage of hand sanitizers against germs

…And much more.

So, without further ado, let's begin proper.

# Chapter 1

## The ABC of Hand Sanitizers

Hand sanitizers were developed for use after handwashing or for times when there is no availability of soap and water.

If you have been in a child's play area, then you must have witnessed how mothers reach for their purse to grab their hand sanitizers as their children come off the play equipment, where each child is given a dab of sanitizer to rub against their hands to disinfect the germs transferred to their skin – in the hope that this practice keeps the children, and their families healthier. Or is it one of those days in late fall when you are stuck at home and covered in each blanket you own, downing bowl after bowl of soup, then having to regret every handshake you gave over the past week, wishing you took necessary steps to put an effective hand sanitizing procedure in place. Well, with the current global pandemic, that time has come for you to put a touchpoint cleaning procedure in place such as handwashing and sanitizing procedures.

## Hand Sanitizer and Its Importance

Hand sanitizers, also referred to as hand rub is a liquid or gel that is applied to the hands to destroy common pathogens or infectious agents or simply, germs, i.e., disease-causing micro-organisms such as virus and bacteria.

In general,

- Hand sanitizers are not only convenient and portable especially when we are unable to wash our hands with soap and water whenever we need to disinfect our hands, but they are also easy to use
- Several studies show that there is a reduced risk of spreading gastrointestinal (stomach) and respiratory infection (e.g., influenza) among families who use hand sanitizers
- Most commercially made hand sanitizers (alcohol and alcohol-free) are made up of compounds

such as glycerol that help prevent skin dryness and irritation.

**Hand Sanitizers Vs. Hand Washing**

Hand sanitizers provide an effective and convenient way through which your hands can be cleaned if soap and water are not available, and your hands are not covered with visible dirt, grease, or chemicals such as pesticides and heavy metals. A 2019 ruling by the Food and Drug Administration (FDA) states that a product can be referred to as a hand sanitizer if it is made up of ethyl alcohol (alternatively called ethanol), Isopropyl alcohol (isopropanol) or benzalkonium chloride as the active ingredient. Any other ingredients that do not comprise these three have shown little to no evidence of being effective at killing germs and have not won the approval of the FDA.

Nonetheless, when it comes to preventing the spread of infectious diseases such as the infamous COVID-19, really and truly, nothing beats the good old-fashioned method of handwashing. Knowing when best to wash your hands, and when to turn to hand sanitizers is vital to protecting yourself not only from the novel coronavirus but other illnesses such as the common cold and seasonal flu (e.g., influenza A virus). The US Centers for Disease Control and Prevention (CDC) and the WHO recommends that whenever possible, handwashing with soap and water should be adopted as the first line of defense against germs because it helps destroy the amount of all types of germs found on the hands. However, if soap and water are not readily available or accessible, and your hands are not covered with visible dirt, grease, or chemicals, the next best option, according to CDC and WHO is using a hand sanitizer with an alcohol concentration of at least 60 percent – this not only kills the germs (including the coronaviruses) but also helps prevent its spread to others. However, not all types of germs are destroyed even with a hand sanitizer of 60 percent alcohol or above. For certain types of germs such as norovirus (not to be confused with coronavirus), Cryptosporidium (a parasite that can cause diarrhea), and Clostridium difficile (a bacteria that causes bowel and diarrhea problems), studies show that handwashing is much effective in removing such germs than using hand sanitizers.

## Alcohol-Based Sanitizers Vs. Alcohol-Free Sanitizers

Depending on the active ingredient used, hand sanitizers are classified as either alcohol-based or alcohol-free sanitizers.

- Alcohol-based sanitizers are unarguably known to kill most micro-organisms or germs. Alcohol-based sanitizers are primarily made up of about 60% to 95% alcohol, usually in the form of ethanol, isopropanol, or n-propanol. At these concentrations of alcohol, the protein (which is vital for the survival and multiplication of micro-organisms) composition in certain micro-organisms is immediately destroyed, thus effectively neutralizing the micro-organisms.

Hand sanitizers below 60 percent of alcohol are found only to reduce the growth of germs and are less effective at destroying it.

- Alcohol-free sanitizers are primarily disinfectants-based, which contains the quaternary ammonium compounds (usually the benzalkonium chloride) or anti-microbial agents, such as triclosan instead of alcohol. Although this can reduce the amount of micro-organisms on the hands, it is, however, less effective than the alcohol-based sanitizers when it comes to destroying micro-organisms.

**Effectiveness of Hand Sanitizers Against Germs**

Although variability in the efficacy of hand sanitizers are prevalent given that not all hand sanitizers are made equally, hand sanitizers nonetheless can help control how infectious diseases are transmitted, especially in situations where there is poor compliance with handwashing. Agencies such as the WHO and CDC promotes the use of alcohol-based hand sanitizers over alcohol-free hand sanitizers due to the safety concerns about the chemicals used in the production of alcohol-free products. Study shows that certain antimicrobial compounds, for example, triclosan which is used in the production of alcohol-free hand sanitizers may interfere with the functioning of the endocrine system. Based on the mounting concerns over triclosan in 2014, authorities in the European Union (E.U.) thus had to limit its usage in several consumer products across the E.U. member countries. Not only that, alcohol-free disinfectants and antimicrobials can also potentially result in the development of anti-microbial resistance, thus making alcohol-free sanitizers less effective in destroying germs.

In subsequent sections of this book, I would focus only on alcohol-based hand sanitizers and how it can be prepared to satisfy the required alcohol volume or concentration.

**What Germs Can Alcohol-Based Hand Sanitizer Kill?**

According to the CDC, an alcohol-based hand sanitizer that satisfies the alcohol volume or concentration requirement can not only reduce the amount of microbes (same as micro-organisms or germs) on your hands but also help destroy a variety of disease-causing agents or pathogens on your hands, such as the SARS-CoV-2 (severe acute respiratory coronavirus 2), colloquially known as coronavirus or COVID-19. Alcohol-based hand sanitizers are also effective at killing many types of bacteria, which include but are not limited to:

- Methicillin-Resistant Staphylococcus Aureus (MRSA), an infection caused by the Staphylococcus bacteria and resistant to many antibiotics, and;
- Escherichia coli (a bacterium that can produce bloody diarrhea).

Also, alcohol-based hand sanitizers are effective in destroying many viruses, including the hepatitis A virus, Middle East respiratory syndrome coronavirus (MERS-CoV), rhinovirus, HIV, and the influenza A virus.

However, certain types of germs cannot be destroyed by even the best alcohol-based hand sanitizers, most notably:

- Norovirus
- Cryptosporidium and;
- Clostridium difficile (also known as C. diff)

Nonetheless, the effectiveness of alcohol-based hand sanitizers in destroying germs relies on many factors, vis-à-vis how it is applied (e.g., the quantity used, the length of exposure, the frequency of use), and whether the particular infectious agents found on the hands are susceptible to the active ingredient of the hand sanitizer. The general rule of thumb of alcohol-based hand sanitizers requires that it is rubbed thoroughly over the surfaces of the finger and hand for at least 30 seconds, followed by total air-drying. In addition, hand sanitizers may not work properly if your hands are visibly dirty or greasy. In such a case, you should opt for handwashing instead of hand sanitizer.

Also, bear in mind that hand sanitizers do expire, which by industry-standard is about two to three years from the date of production if kept in proper condition; this is because when the alcohol in the mixture evaporates over a while, and if it goes below 60 percent, the solution becomes ineffective against germs.

**DIY Hand Sanitizer Benefits**

There is no doubt that some commercial hand sanitizers do their job in destroying germs such as bacteria and viruses; however, not all commercial hand sanitizers are effective enough in destroying germs. As a matter of fact, some commercial hand sanitizers are made up of as little as 57% alcohol, thus making homemade products more suitable to opt for, especially if done right. Also, a good hand sanitizer should contain other ingredients that can hydrate your skin, but in all honesty, do we really take note of each word written on commercial product labels? And to be frank, when armed with the right knowledge in making homemade sanitizers especially in times of scarcity of commercial hand sanitizers, you become more cautious and aware of what to do and not do when making your own hand sanitizers; giving you more independent control in making hand sanitizers that can not only match that obtained in some commercial products but also exceed their effectiveness. That being said, let's briefly have a look at some of the common benefits of homemade sanitizers.

**More quantity**

Conventionally, most commercial hand sanitizers are sold in small bottles. If used frequently, it may run out before you know it, thus making homemade sanitizers more preferable since it affords you the ability to produce how much quantity you deem desirable to meet your needs and those of your families.

**Saves money**

Being able to make your own hand sanitizer and reuse the bottle allows you to minimize unnecessary expenditures when making a new one.

## Ingredient management

As earlier mentioned, we can't be all too sure or trusting of the quality of ingredients that are used in most commercial hand sanitizing products, making homemade products more desirable to opt for since it allows us to control what compound goes into it.

## Scent option

One of the benefits of homemade hand sanitizers is that it allows you to customize the scent of the essential oils to your desired flavor, especially if you are allergic or sensitive to certain scents, or you can leave them out completely.

## Chemical-free

Most commercial based hand sanitizers are produced using chemical compounds that have been found to either be ineffective against the coronavirus or harmful to the body. One of such compound is the triclosan chemical compound which has been flagged by the FDA as a compound not to be used for over the counter consumer products given its potential potency to cause abnormal endocrine system issues. Another of such compound is benzalkonium chloride, an alcohol substitute used in the production of popular alcohol-free hand sanitizer products such as Germ-X and Purell. However, when it comes to combatting the coronavirus, the CDC notes that this ingredient is less reliable than the alcohol-based products. On the other hand, homemade hand sanitizers do not make use of these chemicals because, with the right knowledge, you are more informed not to include these chemicals when making your own hand sanitizer.

**Are DIY Hand Sanitizers Safe?**

It's no longer news that hand sanitizers were one of the first products of defense against the global pandemic to have flown off the shelves and is still almost impossible to get any online or in stores. This has resulted in many attempting their own DIY versions using recipes available all over the internet, which begs the question, are homemade hand sanitizers really safe?

Going by medical requirements, making your own hand sanitizer is not recommended partly because a proper hand sanitizer recipe is all about the proportions, which understandably is difficult for an average consumer to get right. When the proportions or ingredients become off in your little homemade laboratory;

- It renders the product as ineffective, meaning the sanitizer may not destroy the risk of exposure to germs
- It can lead to skin irritation, injury, or burns, and;
- You can become exposed to hazardous chemicals through inhalation.

Another big red flag is that the tools being used must also be sanitized, which is the whole point of hand sanitizers, and if you do not correctly sanitize the tools, the potency of the final product could be compromised.

In addition to using correctly sanitized tools, the WHO's hand sanitizer recipe (later discussed in subsequent sections) also requires that production facilities be air-conditioned and flame-free (ethanol and Isopropyl alcohol are extremely flammable).

Thus, the recipes described in this book are intended to be used by professionals possessing both the expertise and the resources to make homemade hand sanitizers safely. Homemade hand sanitizer is only recommended in extreme situations when you are not able to wash your hands with soap and water or for the foreseeable future.

Having pointed out all these vital concerns as to why homemade sanitizers might not be entirely safe, especially if you are defaulting in any of the concerns mentioned, proceeding otherwise to making your own hand sanitizers using the recipes discussed in this book must be done with extreme caution and adherence to all safety practices.

# Chapter 2

# Making Homemade Sanitizers

In all honesty, making your own hand sanitizer is quick and easy, typically about 5 minutes, especially if you have familiarized yourself with the necessary procedures and precautions to be adhered to. Also, much if not all of the ingredients and tools that you require to get started are available in the personal care section of most grocery stores, such as Whole Foods Market, pharmacy stores, as well as several online retailers, such as Amazon.

## Hand Sanitizer Tools You Need to Have

Before you get started in making your own hand sanitizer, it is essential to have the basic tools to facilitate this process. The items below are a worthy investment to make if you don't have them at home.

**Mixing Bowl:** Required for mixing all your ingredients. Ideally, one that can hold up to three to five cups of liquid would suffice.

**Measuring Spoon**: Required when adding a specific or small amount of ingredient to the recipe.

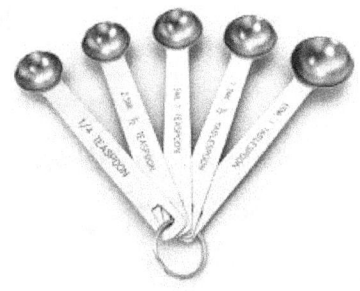

**Measuring Cup or Jug:** A measuring cup or jug is a container (in glass or plastic) with lines printed on its sides used for measuring liquids, which shows the amount it contains. It is very useful when you need to measure ingredients in cup sizes.

**Plastic Funnel:** Required to transfer the finished hand-sanitizing product from the bowl into a bottle. Ideally, a small-sized funnel that fits into the bottle would suffice.

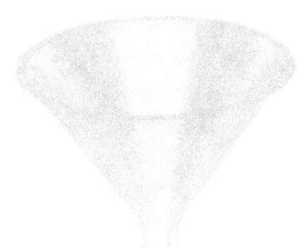

**Nitrile Gloves:** Required to prevent your hands from being burned when making the hand sanitizer.

**PET Pump or Spray Bottles:** Required to store the hand sanitizer once ready. Dark-colored PET pump or spray bottles are most ideal when making your hand sanitizer because when essential oils are added to your hand sanitizer, the dark-colored bottle will prevent degradation of the essential oils from U.V. light.

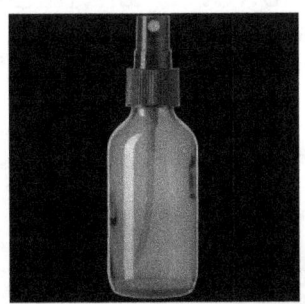 

**Hand Sanitizer Ingredients You Need to Get**

Three main ingredients are typically used when making homemade sanitizer. However, in one or a few recipes I would be discussing shortly, other ingredients may be required either as a substitute to the main ingredient (when the main ingredient is not available) or as an additional ingredient, so be on the lookout for such.

**Isopropyl (Rubbing Alcohol) or Ethanol**

Isopropyl alcohol or ethanol is the main active ingredient in hand sanitizers, and for your homemade sanitizer to be effective in killing germs, especially the coronaviruses, then you must ensure to use undiluted Isopropyl alcohol that has a concentration of 91% percent or above. Ideally, 99% is a common concentration being used; however, anything above 91% will still be effective in killing germs.

Getting hold of Isopropyl can be difficult to come by; however, in such a case, you can opt for pure ethanol instead. Ethanol is the alcohol found in spirits, and one of such recommended spirits is Everclear (a type of grain alcohol), which should be 190 proof (about 95% alcohol volume) for it to be effective in killing germs.

**Aloe Vera Gel**

Isopropyl alcohol needs to be mixed with an emollient, such as aloe vera, which is necessary to add moisture to your hands to soften or soothe your skin else, the Isopropyl alcohol will not only dry out your hands but will also get it cracked or burned. The same applies if you don't use enough aloe vera gel; hence, the need to use the right ratio.

Nonetheless, the ratio you need to make an effective germ-busting hand sanitizer relies on the percentage of alcohol used and the most notable ratio is 2:1

For example, if the Isopropyl alcohol you are using has a concentration of 91%, then the ratio of alcohol to aloe vera will be 2:1, e.g., 3 tbsp of alcohol to 1.5 tbsp of aloe vera, or 2 cups of alcohol to 1 cup of aloe vera gel, the same ratio applies when using 99% Isopropyl alcohol.

Vegetable glycerin can also be used in the absence of aloe vera. Both are used as moisturizers for the hands.

**Essential Oils**

While adding essential oils to your mixture is optional, however, if you detest the smell of alcohol and need to add some fragrance to the mixture that has a germ-busting characteristic, then adding essential oils is your best bet. However, when it comes to hand sanitizers, there a few essential oils amongst the varieties that can be used both as fragrance and germ-busting. One such is the tee tree essential oils, which, by far, is the most recommended essential oil to use for hand sanitizer. According to Medical News Today, the properties of tea tree oil comes with antibacterial features as well as anti-inflammatory, anti-fungal, and antiviral features properties. While there is limited research on the viruses the tea tree essential oil can combat successfully, it is thought to combat the pathogens that are associated with acne, staphylococci, micrococci, Enterococcus faecalis, and Pseudomonas aeruginosa. Lavender, eucalyptus and cinnamon, just like the tee tree, are yet another common essential oil with antiviral, antibacterial, and anti-fungal features. Other popular brands of essential oils are lemon, sweet or wild orange, rosemary, clove, thyme, and peppermint. Whichever type of essential oil you decide to use, caution should be applied because some fragrances could cause an allergic reaction. For example, the lemon essential oil, when used, can cause a phototoxic skin reaction.

**Hand Sanitizer Ingredient You Must Not Use**

It is a known fact that the internet is awash with several recipes on how to make your own hand sanitizer. However, not all the ingredients being recommended online are ideal for making hand sanitizers, especially if you are out to make a hand sanitizer that can kill the coronaviruses. Two of such commonly recommended ingredients you must not use in making your hand sanitizers are vodka and witch hazel.

**Vodka**

Vodka is one common ingredient that most recipes for homemade hand sanitizers recommend in the absence of Isopropyl. Most U.S. vodka comes in the standard 80 Proof, which would give about 40% undiluted alcohol concentration. However, some vodka if you can get hold of them also come in 120 proof, about 60% undiluted alcohol concentration, nonetheless, this is still not suitable for use in making your own hand sanitizer especially because you would most likely dilute this concentration with aloe vera, or glycerin which would further reduce the concentration to less than 60% of the WHO and CDC recommendation. Additionally, the

FDA has only approved the use of USP grade ingredients for making hand sanitizers, and vodka is not a USP grade certified alcohol.

**Witch Hazel**

Witch hazel is a tree-like plant that is indigenous to North America and some parts of Asia. According to the National Institutes of Health (NIH), the extract is gotten from the bark or leaves of the plant and mostly used as an astringent to relieve mild skin irritations such as bites from insect and minor cut or scrapes. This is due to its richness in tannins (compounds found in plants, seeds, bark, and leaves, known to possess some anti-microbial and anti-inflammatory properties), thus its popularity as an ingredient in skincare products.

But does witch hazel actually kill germs?

According to Amesh A. Adalja, a senior scholar of infectious disease at the Johns Hopkins Center for Health Security, "although witch hazel contains chemical compounds that can shrink or constrict body tissues, it is unreliable in killing germs due to the absence of evidence that ascertains its effectiveness as an antiseptic."

This means that witch hazel should not be used as the single germ-bursting ingredient in hand sanitizing solutions, especially those with claims to destroy the coronaviruses, says Rajeev Fernando, M.D., an infectious disease expert in Southampton, New York.

In other words, the many ingredients available on the internet that uses witch hazel in the making of hand sanitizers will not be effective against germs.

Also, the mixing of bleach and ammonia should not be attempted because doing so produces a toxic gas called chloramine, which could lead to chest pain and shortness of breath. Besides, bleach and vinegar should also not be mixed to produce hand sanitizers because it can produce chlorine gas that causes coughing, burning, breathing problems, and watery eyes.

**Safety Precautions for Making Your Hand Sanitizers**

According to Jagdish Khubchandani, an associate professor of health science at Ball State University, making your hand sanitizer at home requires that you adhere strictly to these tips:

- Hand sanitizers should be made in a clean space, and all countertops should be wiped with a diluted bleach solution prior to the production process.
- Hands must be washed thoroughly before making the hand sanitizer.
- Make use of a clean spoon, mixing bowl, whisk, glass, or spray bottles by washing these items thoroughly before their usage.
- Ensure the alcohol in the final product is not diluted below the recommended 60% concentration
- All ingredients should be thoroughly mixed until they are well blended.
- The mixture should not be touched with your hands until it is ready for use.

- Your homemade production facility or laboratory should be air-conditioned and flame-free (ethanol and Isopropyl alcohol are extremely flammable). Also, if it comes in contact with your hands, it will burn your skin, hence, ensure to wear nitrile gloves.
- All homemade sanitizers should be properly labeled to prevent anyone from mistakenly ingesting it.

## **A Short message from the Author:**

Hey, I hope you are enjoying the book? I would love to hear your thoughts!

Many readers do not know how hard reviews are to come by and how much they help an author.

I would be incredibly grateful if you could take just 60 seconds to write a short review on the product page of this book, even if it is a few sentences!

Thanks for the time taken to share your thoughts!

Your review will genuinely make a difference for me and help gain exposure for my work.

Your review will genuinely make a difference for me and help gain exposure for my work.

## Recipes For Homemade Hand Sanitizers

Besides the alcohol used in each recipe, other ingredients are employed to help moisturize your hands and make it smell nice. Note that the proportion of ingredients used in the recipes below all amounts to a final alcohol content that is around 60% and above, which is the recommendation by the WHO and CDC.

Without further ado, let's proceed.

## The WHO Hand Sanitizer Formula

The WHO's recipe for hand sanitizer is primarily used for local production where the production facility is WHO compliant, and not for homemade preparation. However, the recipe below has been scaled down for homemade usage.

To make 1 1/3 cups of hand sanitizer, mix the ingredients below in a mixing bowl that can accommodate three to five cups of liquid

**Ingredients:**

- 1 cup of 99% Isopropyl alcohol or 1 cup plus 4 teaspoons of 91% Isopropyl alcohol
- 1 tablespoon of 3% hydrogen peroxide (needed to destroy the spores of several bacterias in your ingredients and not on your hands)
- 1 teaspoon of 98% glycerin
- Boiled cold water or sterile distilled water

**Directions:**

- Pour the alcohol, peroxide, and glycerin into a mixing bowl, then add sufficient water to bring the quantity to a total of 1 1/3 cups. Mix properly.
- Use a funnel to pour the finished sanitizer into a spray bottle and label accordingly.

**Note:** Because water was used in the preparation, the final product would have less of a gel consistency, hence the need to use a spray bottle.

The final alcohol concentration of this WHO formula is 75%, making it very effective in killing germs such as the novel coronavirus.

**Simple Standard Hand Sanitizer**

This recipe is one of the most common types of recipes out there, easy to make in no time.

**For 91% Isopropyl alcohol:**

**Ingredients:**

- 2/3 cups of 91% Isopropyl alcohol
- 1/3 cup of 100% pure aloe vera gel
- 10 drops of tea tree or lavender essential oil or both

**For 99% Isopropyl alcohol:**

**Ingredients:**

- 3/4 cups of 99% Isopropyl alcohol
- 1/4 cup of 100% pure aloe vera gel
- 10 drops of tea tree or lavender essential oil or both

**Directions:**

Pour the alcohol and the aloe vera gel into a bowl, then add the drops of essential oils. Mix properly using a spoon or spatula.

1. Use a funnel to pour the finished sanitizer into a 2-ounce pump bottle and label accordingly.

**Vitamin E Oil Hand Sanitizer**

This hand sanitizer recipe is made from ingredients with antibacterial, antiviral, and anti-fungal properties, which are all good for the skin. However, the vitamin E oil used nourishes the skin, keeping it hydrated and clean, and also helps preserve the sanitizer.

**Ingredients:**

- 12 teaspoons of 190 proof Everclear (95% alcohol) or higher Isopropyl alcohol

- 10 drops of lavender essential oil
- 6 drops of lemongrass essential oil
- 25 drops of tea tree essential oil
- 6 teaspoons of aloe vera gel
- 1 teaspoon of vitamin E oil

**Direction:**

1. Mix the essential oils and vitamin E oil in a mixing bowl.
2. Pour the alcohol into the mixture and mix, then add the aloe vera gel, mixing properly
3. Transfer the sanitizer to a 2-ounce spray bottle and shake gently before using it. Label accordingly.

**Kid-Friendly Hand Sanitizers By Age Group**

The essential oils used in this recipe are considered kid-friendly, which is why I am comfortable sharing this recipe with you. If you want a cheap, safe, and effective way of making a homemade essential oil hand sanitizer not only for your children but for yourself, then the recipes shared below is your best bet. Whether it's the season of cold or flu, your kids returning to school, or you simply want to protect yourself and kids from the global coronavirus pandemic, and other germs, the below recipes would serve your kids best.

## Citrus Mint Hand Sanitizer

This hand sanitizer recipe uses a mix of antibacterial, antiviral, anti-microbial, and anti-fungal essential oil properties to kill most germs on the hands. This hand sanitizer is appropriate for kids age 10 and up, and should not be used on kids below 10 years old.

**Ingredients:**

- 4 teaspoon of 190 proof Everclear (95% alcohol)
- 1 tsp of aloe vera gel
- 1 tsp of unscented Castille soap
- 5 drops of rosemary essential oil
- 3 drops of lemon essential oil
- 2 drops of peppermint essential oil

**Directions:**

1. Fill a 1-ounce spray bottle with the alcohol and essential oils. Shake properly and allow it to sit undisturbed for some hours so that the alcohol can dissolve as many of the essential oils as possible.
2. After a couple of hours, the aloe vera and Castille soap should be added into the spray bottle, cap the bottle, and shake thoroughly. Label accordingly.

**Lavender-Tea Tree "Little Tykes" Hand Sanitizer**

This hand sanitizer recipe makes use of a mix of two of the most gentle and safest essential oils in a dilution that is appropriate for kids aged 2 – 6 years. This should not be used for kids below 2 years old.

**Ingredients:**

- 4 teaspoon of 190 proof Everclear (95% alcohol)
- 1 tsp of aloe vera gel
- 1 tsp of unscented Castille soap

- 2 drops of lavender essential oil
- 1 drop of tea tree essential oil

**Note:** For directions on how to mix, follow the same directions highlighted just above

## Thieves Hand Sanitizer

The thieves hand sanitizer below comes in two recipes that are suitable for two categories of age group.

**For children 6 months and above:**

This hand sanitizer recipe can be used on children aged 6 months and above. It should not be used on children below 6 months.

**Ingredients:**

- 4 teaspoon of 190 proof Everclear (95% alcohol)
- 1 tsp of aloe vera gel
- 1 tsp of unscented Castille soap
- 5 drops of cinnamon leaf essential oil

- 3 drops of sweet orange essential oil
- 2 drops of pine essential oil

**For children 10 years old and above:**

This hand sanitizer is for children 10 years old and above. It should not be used on children below 10 years.

**Ingredients:**

- 4 teaspoons of 190 proof Everclear (95% alcohol)
- 1 tsp of aloe vera gel
- 1 tsp unscented Castille soap
- 6 drops of thieves essential oil blend

**Note:** For directions on how to mix, follow the same directions highlighted just above.

**Glycerin-Based Hand Sanitizer**

The essential oils used in this recipe are also considered kid-friendly with glycerin substituting for aloe vera.

**Ingredients:**

- 3-4 tablespoons of 190 proof Everclear (95% alcohol) or higher Isopropyl alcohol
- 1/2 teaspoon of glycerin
- 20 drops of tea tree essential oil*
- 10 drops of spruce essential oil**
- 6 drops of lemon essential oil***

**Direction:**

1. Mix the glycerin and the essential oils in a mixing bowl and add it to a 2-ounce spray bottle.
2. Pour in the alcohol to a level where the bottle is almost full, then cover the bottle with its cap and shake properly to combine the ingredients.
3. Gently shake before using it. Label accordingly

**Note:**

*This is about 2% dilution. A dilution of 5-15% is deemed safe for skincare.

**This is about 1% dilution.

\*\*\*This is about 0.5% dilution. Dilution below 2% causes no photo-toxicity, with up to 5% dilution considered safe for skincare.

If you don't want to purchase the individual essential oils, you can use a kid-safe essential oil blend, like the Germ Destroyer from Plant Therapy. If you decide to go this route, you would have to follow the dilution direction shared on Plant Therapy's product page.

## Chapter 3

## Hand Hygiene Practice

Hand hygiene entails the practice of cleaning your hands with soap and water or with an alcohol-based hand rub, such as hand sanitizer. The purpose of hand hygiene is for the removal of grease, dirt, or other unwanted substances that could result in the spread of many diseases. For example, people can be infected with respiratory diseases such as influenza or the common cold, if for example, they do not wash their hands properly before touching their eyes, nose, or mouth. When performed correctly, hand hygiene results in not only the reduction of micro-organisms or germs on the hands but also destroys many germs that are found on the hands, thus preventing its spread to others.

**Why Is It important?**

A good hand hygiene practice is one of the most effective ways to prevent the spread of infections such as the coronavirus and other infections earlier discussed in this book. The truth is most infections amongst people are caused by spreading germs from person-to-person. Even though your hands may look clean, they can still be a carrier of germs, and the reason for this is because germs are so small that you won't be able to see them, making it so easy to spread these germs to others without realizing it. That is why washing your hands regularly is highly recommended, not just when it's covered with visible grease or dirt. Using alcohol-based hand sanitizers where water and soap are not immediately accessible is also recommended. However, this should not be used as a substitute for handwashing, which is by far the most effective way to keep your hands free from germs and disease spreading agents.

## Handwashing the Right Way

Many of us hardly pay attention to how we wash our hands; still, I get a strong feeling that this narrative is changing maybe as a result of the current global pandemic where proper hand hygiene is being emphasized as very essential to curbing the spread of the virus. It is also noteworthy to mention that your hands should be washed:

- after you cough, sneeze or blow your nose
- before, during and after preparing food
- after going to the toilet or changing a nappy
- when your hands are visibly dirty
- after smoking
- after handling or patting animals
- before and after taking care of someone who is sick
- before eating and;
- after touching surfaces that could be contaminated

This list is not exhaustive; however, depending on your situation, always ensure to wash your hands, make it a ritual.

But most importantly is that the aforementioned be done the right way else it counters the purpose, which is to reduce and destroy the germs on your hands and curtail its spread to others. To this effect, the CDC has released a guideline with specific instructions on the most effective way to wash your hands. This is what they recommend:

1. Always make use of clean, running water
2. Washing your hands with warm water and soap is the gold standard for hand hygiene, as well as preventing the spread of infectious diseases. When the hands are washed with warm water (not cold water) and soap, it removes oils from the hands that may harbor micro-organisms.
3. Your hands should first be wet with water, then lather your hands with soap.
4. Your hands should be rubbed together with the soap for about 20 seconds or more, scrubbing the

back of your hands, under your nails and between your fingers.

5. Rinse your hands with water and use air or a clean towel to dry.

**Using Hand Sanitizers Effectively**

There are two things to note when using hand sanitizer. First, it needs to be rubbed into your skin until your hands become dry. Secondly, if your hands are greasy or dirty, it needs to be washed with soap and water before applying hand sanitizer.

With that in mind, the below tips are how to use hand sanitizers effectively.

1. Apply enough sanitizer to the palm of one hand.
2. Rub your hands together thoroughly, making sure that the entire surface of your hands, the back of your hands, under your nails and between your fingers are well covered.
3. Keep rubbing for about 30 to 60 seconds or until your hands become dry. Most times, it takes about 60 seconds and, in other cases, a little longer for the hand sanitizer to kill most germs.

# Conclusion

Congratulations on having to transit the lines of this book from start to finish.

In this book, I have provided you with the most valid information that you need to safely make your own hand sanitizer in 5 minutes amidst the scarcity and overpriced hand sanitizers out there in several online stores, supermarkets, and pharmacies. Not only that, but I have also ensured the recipes shared are compliant with the recommended alcohol concentration that is very effective in destroying most bacteria and viruses, including the COVID-19 virus. The preparation process has also been simplified to make it easy for you to understand and follow through with. Lastly, I have shared important tips you need in practicing hand hygiene, which is all but essential toward combating bacteria and viruses. Therefore, it is my sincere desire that you found great value from the invaluable and simplified insights shared in this book, which I hope you put into action right away.

Given the current global pandemic, I urge you to take full responsibility for your overall health and wellbeing.

I wish you the very best on your journey toward a hygienic lifestyle.

# References

Lindberg, S. (2020, March 23). How to Make Your Own Hand Sanitizer. Retrieved from https://www.healthline.com/health/how-to-make-hand-sanitizer#effectiveness

Rogers, K. (2019, August 22). Hand sanitizer. Retrieved from https://www.britannica.com/topic/hand-sanitizer

Post, T. J. (2020, March 15). COVID-19: Not all hand sanitizers work against it – here's what you should use. Retrieved from https://www.thejakartapost.com/life/2020/03/15/covid-19-not-all-hand-sanitizers-work-against-it-heres-what-you-should-use.html

Jacobs, K. L. (2020, March 31). Hand Sanitizer (WHO Formula) –. Retrieved from https://www.agardenforthehouse.com/2020/03/hand-sanitizer-who-formula/

Hein, A. (2020, March 17). Coronavirus panic buying prompts DIY hand sanitizer: Avoid mixing these ingredients. Retrieved from https://www.foxnews.com/health/coronavirus-panic-buying-diy-hand-sanitizer-avoid-mixing-ingredients

Marr, K. (2020, March 19). Homemade Hand Sanitizer Spray (Kid-Friendly). Retrieved from https://livesimply.me/homemade-hand-sanitizer-spray-kid-friendly/

A. (2020, April 6). Homemade Hand Sanitizer for Travel. Retrieved from https://52perfectdays.com/articles/homemade-hand-sanitizer-for-travel/

Meagan Visser. (2020, March 14). Homemade Essential Oil Hand Sanitizer Recipes For Adults & Children. Retrieved from https://www.growingupherbal.com/homemade-essential-oil-hand-sanitizer/

Miller, K. (2020, March 14). Does Witch Hazel Kill Germs? Here's Why It's Not Reliable, According to Doctors. Retrieved from https://www.prevention.com/health/a31344840/does-witch-hazel-kill-germs/

Show Me the Science – When & How to Use Hand Sanitizer in Community Settings. (2020, March 3). Retrieved from https://www.cdc.gov/handwashing/show-me-the-science-hand-sanitizer.html

# PART II

**The 10-Minutes DIY Homemade Face Mask**

A Step By Step Beginners Guide to Make Your Own Protective, Washable, and Reusable Cloth Face Mask With Illustrations Included

## Introduction

It is no surprise that homemade face masks have now become an essential global commodity amidst the current global pandemic crises, most especially after the WHO and CDC changed its guidelines that required that everyone should wear some form of cloth face-covering when moving around in public places to prevent the spread of COVID-19. This announcement has resulted in a surge of consumers swooping in on supermarkets and online stores to purchase face masks, most notably, the medical face masks and the N95 respirators, which are both reserved for use by healthcare professionals. This has led to an increased scarcity of this all too important commodity, which is mostly needed in hospitals, thus calling for consumers to seek out alternative measures in making their own face masks from home. As a result of the ever-increasing demand for face masks, the internet has thus become awash with several Do-It-Yourself homemade face mask guides, many of which do not take into cognizance the recommended fabrics and steps that must be adhered if the aim is to protect the wearer from the coronavirus. Nonetheless, it is surprisingly easy to make a DIY face mask using materials you most likely have at home; however, not everyone has the experience in using the sewing machine to make a face mask, and if this is you, then not to worry because this book does not only cater for people with experience in using the sewing machine but also people with no experience using the sewing machine, threads and needle. With this book, simplified using the most easy-to-understand language, you are on your way to making your own face mask in 10 minutes or less from the comfort of your home even if you have no clue where to start from.

At the end of this book, you will:

- Gain a deeper understanding of what face mask is and its importance against viruses and toxic particles.
- Be enlightened on the different types of face masks used for protection against COVID-19, the efficacy of each type of masks against virus infections, as well as when and who should use them.
- Know how face masks work in protecting you from viruses and toxic particles.
- Understand the real benefits of making your own face mask from home.
- Know the best fabrics to use if you want to make a reusable homemade face mask.
- Know why you should not use some of the commonly recommended fabrics for your face mask.
- Uncover all you need to get started in making your own face mask with the sewing and no-sewing methods, such as the material lists, measurements and cut list in inches for adults

and kids, as well as the step by step instructions to follow.
- Be familiar with the best practice for handling face mask, either when wearing or removing a face mask to stay protected against the viruses and toxic particles that you mask may habor without your knowledge.

…and much more.

So, without further ado, let's begin proper

# Chapter 1

# The ABC of Face Mask

In late 2019, a novel coronavirus emerged in China, which has since spread rapidly throughout the world. This novel coronavirus is called severe acute respiratory syndrome coronavirus 2 (SARS-CoV-2), and the disease that it causes is called coronavirus disease, colloquially called COVID-19.

While it is common for people with COVID-19 to experience light illness, others may also experience difficulty in breathing, respiratory failure or even pneumonia. It is known that older individuals, as well as people with underlying health conditions, are at higher risk for severe illness from COVID-19. It is to this effect that the World Health Organization (WHO) and the Centers for Disease Control and Prevention (CDC) have called for the practice of safe health against this disease, one of such being the use of face masks to prevent infection, others are regular handwashing with soap and water or in its absence, the use of hand sanitizer as well practicing social distancing.

## What is Face Mask

Face masks are one tool used for curbing the spread of diseases. They are loose-fitting masks that typically cover the nose and mouth, with ear loops, ties or bands behind the head.

Face mask protects the nose and mouth of the wearer from splashes or sprays of body fluids. When a person coughs, talks or even sneezes, there is the tendency that tiny drops of such can be released into the atmosphere, with the potential to infect others. Wearing a face mask by someone who is ill can reduce the number of germs that are released, thus protecting other people from becoming sick.

But, are face masks really that effective, and if yes, when should it be worn and by who?

Read on to learn the answers to this question and more.

## Types of Face Mask and Recommendations For Usage

When you hear of COVID-19 prevention face masks, there are generally three types of such masks recognized by the WHO and CDC.

Let us explore each of them in a bit more detail below.

**N95 Respirator**

A respirator is a personal protective equipment (PPE), which, when worn, prevents health hazards, such as inhaling of aerosol particles (e.g., dust, mist, and smoke). It also provides protection to the wearer from airborne infectious agents such as viruses and bacteria, an example of which are the coronavirus, H1N1, SARS, etc. An example of such a respirator is the N95, which is a more tight-fitting face mask, capable of not only filtering out 95 percent of microscopic particles, but also, splashes, sprays, and large droplets, including viruses and bacteria. This type of mask is not meant for use by the general public. They are to be worn:

- Exclusively by health care professionals attending to patients having respiratory infections such as cough and cold as well as patients under investigation.

- While entering rooms of confirmed or suspected COVID-19 patients.
- While retrieving clinical specimens, or soiled medical supplies and equipment or whenever a health care professional come in contact with potentially contaminated environmental surfaces.

This respirator is generally oval in shape and designed to provide a tight seal to your face, with elastic bands helping to hold it to your face firmly. Some types may include an exhalation valve as an attachment to help with breathing and the buildup of heat and humidity.

N95 respirators are not one-size-fits-all and must be fit-tested before usage to ensure a proper seal is formed, else, you won't receive adequate protection. And even after being fit-tested, wearers of N95 respirators must always perform a seal check any time they put one on.

For respirators to be used for commercial consumption, they must meet the NIOSH (National Institute for Occupational Safety and Health) standards in the US, and the European standard EN 149: 2001 in Europe.

## Medical (Surgical) Face Mask

Medical face masks are a disposable medical device and loose-fitting masks that provide cover for your nose, mouth, and chin, thus:

- Protecting you from sprays, splashes and large-particle droplets
- Preventing the spread of potentially infectious secretions of the respiratory tract from the wearer to others

When a medical mask is worn by a caregiver, the patient and his or her environment (air, surfaces, surgical site, etc.) are protected. Studies conducted shows that medical professional using medical face masks correctly are 80% less risky of being infected than those who don't. On the other hand, when a contagious patient wears it, the patient is prevented from contaminating his or her surroundings and environment.

Medical masks come in different designs but are often flat and rectangular in shape with folds, and with a metal strip at its top that can be formed to your nose.

Medical masks are supported by elastic bands or long, straight ties that keep the mask in place while it's worn, which are either looped to the back of the ears or tied around the head.

For medical masks to be used for commercial consumption, they must comply with the United States American Society for Testing and Materials (ASTM) standards, and in Europe, it must satisfy the European standard EN 14683

Both the N95 respirators and medical masks are critical supplies that the CDC recommends to be reserved for healthcare workers that work with infectious patients. However, this is not the case, as it is evident that the rapid spread of COVID-19 throughout the world has led many people to purchase medical masks to keep at home, in addition to the imbalance in the demand and supply of N95 respirators. These gaps have resulted in the making of homemade face mask as an alternative and additional measure of protection from the virus.

## Homemade Cloth Face Mask

To curb the spread of coronavirus by people without symptoms, the CDC now recommends that everyone wears cloth face masks, such as homemade face masks while in public places where social distancing of up to six-feet is difficult to maintain, e.g. supermarkets and pharmacies. This recommendation is alongside the continued adherence to proper hygiene practices.

Healthcare workers who make use of homemade face masks as opposed to N95 respirators or surgical masks are advised to apply extreme caution, which is recommended to be used in combination with a face shield covering the whole front and sides of the face and extending to the chin or below.

Two ways wearing a face mask helps prevent people from being infected are:

- By blocking the inhalation of the virus through most airborne droplets.
- By preventing the wearer from touching their mouths and noses.

## Are Face Masks Effective Against Virus Infection?

SARS-CoV-2 can be spread from person to person through small respiratory droplets, which are generated when a person infected with the virus exhales, coughs, or sneezes. A person can then contract this virus when these droplets are breathed in. Also, respiratory droplets housing the virus can be transferred to several objects or surfaces. When these contaminated objects or surfaces are touched, and you thereafter touch your eyes, nose, or mouth, it can also lead to infection.

But does wearing a face mask help prevent the spread of viruses, such as the flu or SARS-CoV-2?

Let's take a look at what the experts have to say on this subject.

In the case of COVID-19, the CDC mentions that simple face coverings or masks can lower its spread, thus recommending that people should wear a cloth face covering to cover their nose and mouth when in a public setting, and also recommends healthcare workers wear face masks when handling with patients with the flu. This is in addition to social distancing, regular hand cleaning or hand washing and other everyday preventive actions.

Additionally, a study conducted in 2013 looked at how face masks could help limit the spread of seasonal flu from infected persons when they exhale small droplets housing the virus. In all, it was found that wearing face masks resulted in more than a threefold reduction in how much virus was sprayed into the air by infected persons.

Another study that was analyzed from the data of thousands of Japanese schoolchildren found that vaccination and wearing a face mask reduced the likelihood of contracting seasonal influenza. And more importantly, researchers discovered that the rate of contracting the flu was reduced when face masks were worn alongside proper hand hygiene. This thus leads to the conclusion that although face masks help reduce the spread of flu and the coronavirus, regular washing of the hands remains an essential element in stopping the spread of the viruses. That being said, are all face masks then equally effective at preventing the spread of viruses such as the coronavirus? Let's have a look at the recommendations from experts per the effectiveness of the three major types of face masks against the novel coronavirus.

**N95 Respirator**

N95 respirator masks certified for use by the CDC and NIOSH, are designed to protect the wearer from large and small particles in the air, such as viruses as well as smaller respiratory droplets, such as those containing SARS-CoV-2. The name stems from the fact that they can filter 95 percent of airborne particles, according to the CDC. They are also used when painting or handling likely toxic materials.

N95 masks are mostly used by healthcare workers to protect them against airborne infectious diseases, most notably, the COVID-19. Unlike the regular face masks such as medical masks, respirators protect against large and small particles. Overall, N95 masks are considered more effective at preventing the spread of the flu and coronavirus when compared to medical face masks.

For N95 respirators to be effective at preventing viruses, it must form a perfect seal so that no gaps can allow airborne viruses to pass through.

**Medical Mask**

Medical (surgical) face masks are relatively loose-fitting, disposable masks approved for use by the Food and Drug Administration (FDA) as medical devices, and which are often worn by doctors, dentists, and nurses while treating patients.

These masks prevent the escape of large droplets of bodily fluids (that may house viruses or other germs) via the nose and mouth. Likewise, they protect against splashes and sprays from other persons, e.g., those from sneezes and coughs. However, the average masks bought at the local drugstore are insufficient to filter out viruses in tiny droplets. For example, medical masks can't protect a person from being infected with SARS-CoV-2. Medical masks do not filter out smaller aerosol particles, and even so, as you inhale, air leakage via the sides of the mask occurs.

For this purpose, experts recommend special masks with a fine mesh capable of capturing microscopic organisms that have to be worn correctly for them to work.

It is important to note when airborne virus particles, from a cough or sneeze, comes in contact with your eyes, masks worn over the face would be unable to protect you from such viruses.

**Homemade Cloth Face Mask**

Homemade cloth face masks used in public settings don't provide the same level of protection as N95 respirators and medical face masks but only offer a small degree of protection. However, when worn by the broader public, they can help reduce the community spread of viruses. This is because they help protect others from being infected by your respiratory droplets (such as sneezes and coughs) if you acquired the coronavirus but without symptoms and vice versa.

The CDC recommends that in addition to using homemade face masks in public settings, social distancing and proper hygiene should likewise be practiced.

**Why You Should Make Your Own Face Mask**

- Making your own face mask from the availability of common materials can be made at the convenience of your home in unlimited supply, especially when you become sick, which will help provide some level of protection to friends and family while you seek medical advice
- Making your own face mask, as well as for family and friends, would help decrease the demand for

limited supplies of commercial medical face masks, which are critically needed by hospitals and nursing homes.
- Homemade face masks can lower the risk of people without symptoms from transmitting the virus via speaking, coughing, or sneezing.
- Homemade face masks, when done right is washable and reusable, thus making them environmentally friendly.

## Reusing and Disposing of Face Mask

Most face masks, by best practice, are designed for one-time use only. Ideally, once a face mask is soiled, or the inner lining becomes moist, such a mask should no longer be used because rarely can they be sterilized for reuse. For example, the WHO recommends that a single-use mask be removed once it is damp from your breath and never reuse it. Under normal circumstances, such masks are disposed of when an infected patient has been tended to by a healthcare professional. However, due to the dwindling supply of face masks, and if you need to use a face mask either because you are sick or taking care of a sick person, then face masks can be reused under certain conditions.

The procedures below details how to reuse and dispose of a face mask across the three major types of COVID-19 face mask.

**Medical Face Mask**

The CDC, in a bid to address the shortage of face masks, released a guideline that addresses the reusability of face masks. One of such is that a medical mask should be used only by the same person and not shared amongst medical professionals, and when not in use, such a mask be stored in a breathable container, like a paper bag. Also, extra measures, as given below, can be taken to further ensure a medical face mask can be reused, given the shortages in its availability.

If the mask is dry and its layers and shape remains intact, it can then be reused for three days. To reuse a medical face mask, simply put it in a zip lock pouch with a desiccated gel. The purpose of the gel is to absorb the moisture, thus keeping the mask dry. On the other hand, if it has been worn by an infected person, it should never be reused but immediately discarded.

## N95 Respirator

According to the CDC guidelines, it is better to wear the respirator for an extended period (such as the whole shift) instead of taking it off then putting it back on. This is because it reduces the number of people touching their faces, which potentially allows the virus to enter their body. It also recommends a clean and breathable container such as a paper bag for storing the N95 respirators, which is to be regularly disposed of, so they don't contaminate your mask later on. The guidelines, however, provide no safe amount of reuses, leaving medical professionals to apply their judgment. Nonetheless, additional steps can be taken to preserve and reuse N95 respirators, as given below.

N95 respirators are to be stored in a closed plastic container when not in use with regular cleansing of the storage container. For the N95 respirator to be reused, a number of steps can be taken.

- The used respirator can be left in the dry atmosphere for about 3-4 days to dry out. The reason for this is that coronavirus requires a host in other to survive. It can survive for up to 48hours on a metal surface, for 72 hours on plastic, and for 72 hours on cardboard. Thus, if the respirator is left to dry for about 3-4 days, the virus would not survive.
- Another way is sterilizing the N95 respirator is by hanging it in the oven (without contacting metal) using a wooden clip for about 30 min at 70 degrees Celsius.

N95 respirators that adhere to the above procedure can be used up to a maximum of 5 times, or alternatively, follow the guidelines made available by the manufacturer.

On the other hand, N95 respirators are to be immediately discarded if:

- It is used during aerosol-generating procedures, i.e., procedures such as coughing, that cause the

release of airborne particles, which can result in the spread of respiratory infections.
- It is contaminated with blood, nasal or respiratory secretions, or other bodily fluids from patients.
- The wearer came in close contact with any patient infected with an infectious disease.

## Homemade Cloth Face Mask

A 2015 study published in the medical journal BMJ Open, advised against the medical use of cloth masks, in contrast with disposable ones. This reason for this is that moisture retention, poor filtration, as well as the reuse of cloth masks could result in an increased risk of healthcare workers being infected. However, individuals using their own cloth masks are required to wash them after each use or regularly machine-wash them. Nonetheless, you should be aware that using a homemade cloth face mask would only be marginally effective at preventing the spread of infectious disease when compared with a medical face mask or an N95 respirator. Still, it is better than having no protection at all.

The WHO also mentioned that heat of 133°F could kill the coronavirus, meaning if you are using a homemade face mask made from cloth, it should be washed properly and frequently after each use with detergent and water, then having it air-dried. This would make such masks reusable after it has been worn.

# Chapter 2

## DIY Homemade Face Mask

Given the current shortage of face masks such as the medical face masks and N95 respirators, which by the way, are reserved for health care professionals, most people have thus been forced to seek out ways in creating homemade face masks with anything from cloth to scarves and bandanas.

Although homemade face masks made from cotton woven fabric are about one-third as effective as medical masks in preventing infection, they are still capable of reducing the number of germs spread by the wearer significantly.

### Best Fabrics For Reusable Homemade Mask

Right off the bat, the best fabric for homemade masks is a tightly woven, 100% cotton fabric such as bedsheets, woven shirts, curtains, or fabric from pillowcases, which are all great options if made totally from cotton. If you have clothing or bedding items at home that are still in good condition, they can be used rather than having to buy new fabric.

On the other hand, it is recommended to avoid knit jersey and T-shirt fabrics, simply because they create holes when stretched, which could allow the virus to pass through.

Besides a pure 100% cotton fabric, a non-fusible nonwoven interface fabric for the filter pocket can also be used. This is also needed to provide an extra layer to block out particles. However, if unavailable, the nonwoven fabric can be substituted for a high-efficiency particulate air (HEPA) vacuum bag filter without fiberglass, which is also good for filtering particles. Still, you must ensure that the HEPA filter is one that is washable and reusable else, you will always have to replace the filters each time you wear the mask.

**Are Fabric Face Masks Really Effective?**

Yes and no.

The CDC advises the use of N95 respirators for the best protection but notes that bandana or scarf be used as a last resort if hospital-approved medical masks are unavailable, especially for medical professionals.

However, at this point in the global pandemic, homemade masks are being made by the broader population as a replacement for bandanas and scarves.

According to the CDC, if you need a mask for yourself or other persons not treating COVID-19 patients, then homemade cloth masks can help minimize the spread of the coronavirus. These fabric masks help best to protect you in places such as pharmacies or grocery stores from asymptomatic persons, where it is difficult to maintain a six-feet distance from other shoppers and works best if worn by everyone else.

## Are Coffee Filters, Paper Towels, and Tissues Effective?

Even though the CDC guidelines for DIY homemade face masks incorporate a coffee filter, Nate Favini, a board-certified internist, remarks that coffee filters, paper towels, and tissues (even in layers) are not very effective at filtering out microscopic particles. Besides, they cants also be washed, thus making it impossible for a face mask made of these materials to be reused. However, this does not imply they can't be used if it so happens to be the only materials at your disposal.

Aside from the weak filtration property of the coffee filters, they can quickly become saturated with moisture, making face masks made with any of these paper materials suitable only for one-time use only. That being said, subsequent sections on making homemade face masks would focus on fabrics that can be washed and reused.

## Making Homemade Face Mask

In subsequent sections, I would discuss in a simple fashion how you can make your own face masks either by sewing or no-sewing methods, especially for those who aren't a seamstress or a seamster.

So, without further ado, let's begin.

## Sewing Method

Research shows that the most effective masks are made of two layers of tightly woven cotton fabric, with an internal pocket filter where additional layers of filtration material can be added if desired. The method described below satisfies this study.

## List of Materials and Tools

- 100% tightly woven cotton fabric
- Elastic or fabric ties (to make strips, use the same cotton fabric, or pre-made bias binding, or strips of cotton jersey) for the ear loop to keep the mask secure on the face
- Nonfusible nonwoven interface filter fabric for an extra layer of protection (or HEPA filter) – optional
- Pipe cleaner, floral wire, or other flexible metal wire for nose cover – optional
- Scissors
- Measuring tape
- Pins or clips
- Sewing machine and thread

## Instructions

## Step 1: Measurement and Cut List

Cotton fabric:

- For adult-sized, cut the fabric into one rectangular shape at 16" long and 8.5" wide
- For child-sized, cut the fabric into one rectangular shape at 14" long and 6.5" wide

Elastic:

- For adult-sized, cut 2 pieces of 7" long (or 8" for larger adult size) elastic ear loop
- For child-sized, cut 2 pieces of 6" long elastic ear loop

Fabric ties, if elastic are not used:

- Cut 4 rectangular pieces of fabric ties each at 18" long and 1.75" wide. If 18" is too long for some people, you can adjust the length accordingly.
- Fold the long sides so that it meets in the middle, then fold again in half to encase the raw edges. To create the ties, stitch down the length of the rectangles along the edge, as shown below.

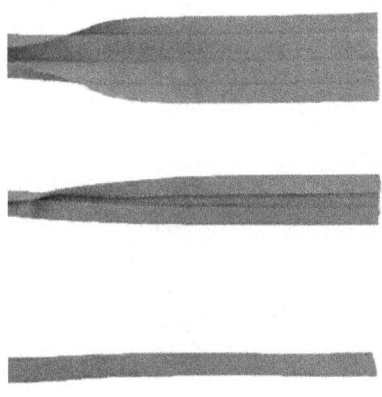

## Step 2: Fold and Sew Along The Top Edge

- Fold the rectangle cotton fabric into half, with the right sides facing each other as shown below

- Sew along the top edge of width 8.5", by using a 5/8" seam (a line where two pieces of fabric are sewn together) allowance and leave a 4" opening at the center of the seam (marked with pins as shown above) for the filter pocket, and to allow the mask to be turned right side out after sewing.

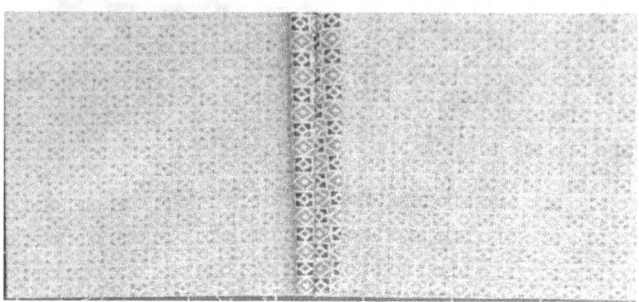

- Turn the fabric so that the seam is centered in the middle of one side, then fold the excess seam allowance under to encase the raw edge of the fabric, then topstitch (as shown below) along the sides of the seam for a neater edge. This is to help prevent the fraying of the fabric when filters are inserted and removed.

**Note:** When topstitching, ensure not to mistakenly stitch the 4" opening at the center of the seam.

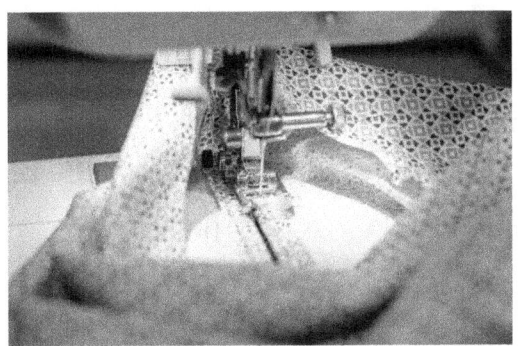

**Step 3: Pin Elastic or Fabric Ties**

If Using Elastic:

- Sandwich the elastic pieces between the two layers of the fabric, then pin one end of the elastic to the top and the other end to the bottom of the sides of the fabric rectangle. This will create the elastic earloop on the outside immediately the mask is turned right side out and pleated.
- Repeat this process on each side to make two ear loops.

**If Using Fabric Ties:**

- If no elastic is available, 4 fabric ties, one in each corner, with each one being 18" long, can likewise be used. One tie in each of the 4 corners should then be sewn. Caution should be applied so as not to catch the ties or the elastic pieces in the side seams when sewing them.

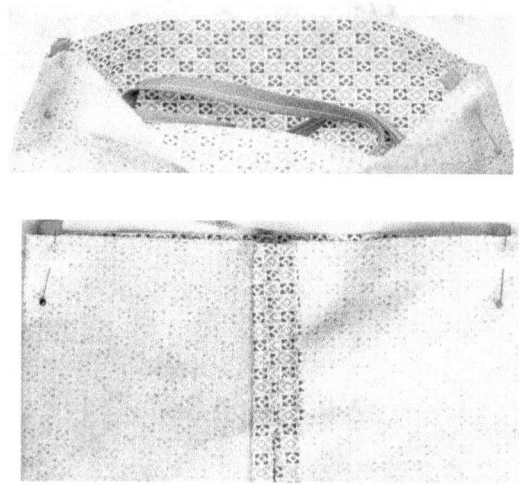

## Step 4: Sew The Sides To Secure The Elastic or Ties

- Using a 3/8" seam allowance, sew the sides of the facemask, backstitch over the elastic or fabric ties to secure them, then trim the corners of the face mask with scissors to make it easier to turn the mask right side out. Be careful not to clip the stitches mistakenly.

- Turn the mask right side out and press with an iron.

## Step 5: Insert a Metal Wire For Nose Cover

- For the mask to fit properly around your nose, cut a 6" piece of pipe cleaner, floral wire, or other flexible wire to make a nose cover.
- Insert the wire via the pocket opening before forming the pleats, and slide it to the very top of the mask. Topstitch around the sides of the wire to keep it in place.

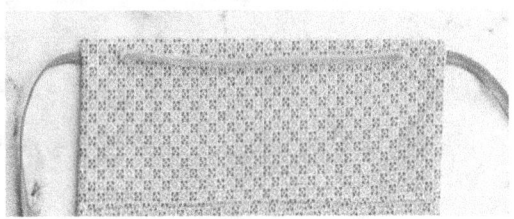

## Step 6: Make The Pleats

- Use a pen to mark the mask with three evenly spaced lines, and use the lines to create evenly spaced 1/2" pleats. Use pins to hold down the folds and ensure all the pleats are facing the same direction.

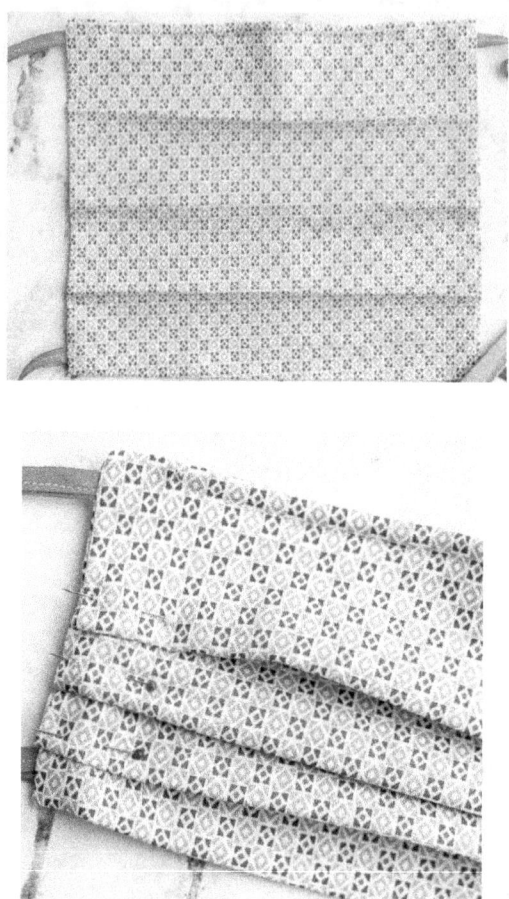

- Sew along the sides of the pleats to secure them. This ensures the pleats open downwards when the mask is worn, thus stopping any particles from being collected into the fold pockets.

**Step 7: Insert The Filter**

- Make a filter for the mask using a non-fusible nonwoven interfacing or HEPA filter without fiberglass. How big this filter would be depends on the size of the filter pocket opening. Cut out the appropriate shape and fit it inside the filter pocket of your mask until it fits in smoothly.
- All the areas that you will need to breathe through should be well covered. The filter does not need to go all through the under of your chin or even the area of your cheeks since the mask presses these areas against your face.

Upon making the mask, it is important that it is sterilized by washing with detergent and water, using a washing machine, or by boiling it in water to kill any inherent germs. Then allow it to dry out either by sun-drying or hanging it in an area with good airflow.

## No-Sewing "Emergency" Method

Making a no-sew face mask is easier than you may be thinking, and a convenient substitute if you can not sew or do not have the proper materials. The no-sew method does not require you to be crafty or to have experience in using the needle and thread. The good news is it takes about 5 minutes to make, all from the supplies you most likely have at home. I have included potential substitutions in the following demonstration should incase you don't have the suggested items.

So, let's begin.

## List of Materials

- 100% tightly woven cotton fabric or a cotton bandana or scarf as recommended by CDC
- Nonfusible nonwoven interface filter fabric for an extra layer of protection (or HEPA filter) – optional
- Pipe cleaner, floral wire, or other flexible metal wire – optional

- Rubber bands, hair ties, or shoelaces

**Instructions**

**Step 1: Prepare Your Fabric**

- Cut and lay out a 20"x 20" or a 22"x 22" square of cotton fabric or any of the substitutes in the material list section above. It has to be either of these measurements so that it's large enough to cover your nose and mouth.
- Lay out flat your chosen fabric on the table, with the patterned side faced down towards the table, and the backside faced upward towards you
- Place the filter in the center of the square (optional)

**Step 2: Make The First and Second Folds**

- For the first fold, fold the top and bottom edge of the fabric so that they converge at the center of your chosen fabric.

- Place a pipe cleaner, floral wire, or other flexible metal wire at the center of the top edge to make a nose cover (optional). This helps the mask fit properly around your nose.
- For the second fold, repeat the same process by folding the top and bottom edge of the fabric. This will create some pleats that will help make the mask fit properly on your face.

**Step 3: Fold The Ends of the Fabric**

- Fold both the right and left sides of your chosen fabric towards the center. A smaller rectangle of folded fabric will now be formed. This will help you to place a rubber band on both sides of the smaller rectangular fabric.

**Step 4: Insert The Rubber Bands**

- Slip in the rubber band at one end of the folded fabric, and another band on the other end. If using hair ties instead, loop it around the end of the fabric. And if using shoelaces, place the center

of the shoelace in the folded fabric and pull the straps tight.
- Tuck the ends of the folds into each other to secure the fabric.

**Step 5: Lift The Mask to Your Face**

- To wear, lift and bring the mask to your mouth, putting the bands or hair ties around your ears to have it secured. For shoelaces, it should be tied behind your head.
- Adjust the mask where necessary, and ensure both your mouth and nose are well covered

## **A Short message from the Author:**

Hey, I hope you are enjoying the book? I would love to hear your thoughts!

Many readers do not know how hard reviews are to come by and how much they help an author.

I would be incredibly grateful if you could take just 60 seconds to write a short review on the product page of this book, even if it is a few sentences!

Thanks for the time taken to share your thoughts!

Your review will genuinely make a difference for me and help gain exposure for my work.

# Chapter 3

# Best Practice For Handling Face Mask

When a face mask becomes moist, it should be removed, replaced, or washed. Product instructions on the use and storage of face mask should always be followed, as well as the procedures on wearing and removing a face mask. If no product instructions are available for wearing and removing a face mask, then you should adhere to the guidelines below.

**Wearing Face Masks The Right Way**

Although face masks can help minimize the spread of the flu and other respiratory viruses, they only do so if worn correctly and regularly.

The guidelines below are to be followed for proper mask-wearing:

1. Your hands should first be cleaned with soap and water or hand sanitizer for at least 20 seconds before touching and wearing a face mask.

2. Ensure no tears or holes are found on either side of the face mask before it is worn.
3. Ensure that you figured the side of the mask that is the top. The top of the mask (typically the side that has a stiff bendable edge) is designed to adjust to the shape of your nose.
4. Ensure that you figured the side of the mask that is the front. This is because the colored side of the mask is usually the front and is designed to be worn from the outside, away from your face, with the white side touching your face. This step typically describes a medical face mask, so you need to determine the front of your homemade face mask.
5. Adjust the stiff edge of the mask to fit into the shape of your nose.
6. Pull the bottom of the mask over your mouth and chin.
7. The instructions below should be followed for the type of ear loops you are using to keep the mask secured on your face.

- Face mask with elastic earloops: Hold the mask by the ear loops, then place a loop around each ear.
- Face mask with ties: The mask should be brought to your nose level, then place the top ties around the crown of your head, securing it with a bow, and likewise, secure the bottom ties with a bow at the nape of your neck.

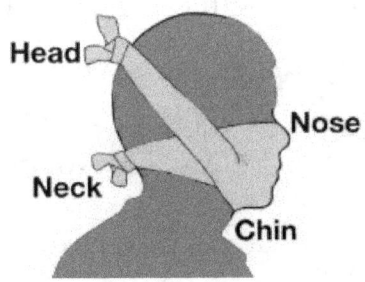

- Face mask with bands: With the mask in your hand, and with its top (the nosepiece) at your fingertips, allow the bands to freely hang below your hands. Then bring the mask to the level of your nose, and pull the top strap around your head so that it is resting over the crown of your head. Likewise, pull the bottom strap around your head so that it is resting at the nape of your neck.

8. The mask should not be touched upon being worn until it is removed, and if touched, rewash your hands or use hand sanitizer.

**Removing Face Masks The Right Way**

While removing a face mask, care should be applied to ensure it is being done the right way. This is because not removing the mask according to best practice puts you at risk of being infected with the flu or other respiratory virus.

The guidelines below are to be followed for proper mask-removal:

1. Your hands should be cleaned with soap and water or with a hand sanitizer before touching the mask.
2. Avoid having to touch the front of the mask, which is more likely to have been contaminated. Only the elastic ear loops, ties, or band should be touched with your hands.

3. The instructions below should be followed for the type of ear loops you are using when removing the face mask

   - Face mask with elastic earloops: Hold both of the elastic ear loops and gently lift and remove the mask.
   - Face mask with ties: The bottom bow should first be untied, followed by the top bow, then gently pull the mask away from your face as the ties are loosened.
   - Face mask with bands: The bottom strap over your head should first be lifted, then pull the top strap over your head, gently pulling the mask away.

4. Follow the procedure in this section of the book, **Reusing and Disposing of Face Mask**, after wearing a medical face mask, respirator, or a homemade cloth face mask to determine how each mask should either be reused or disposed of.
5. Clean your hands with soap and water or with hand sanitizer after discarding the face mask.

# Conclusion

I'd like to thank you and congratulate you for transiting my lines from start to finish.

In this book, I have provided you with the most valid information that you need to safely make your own face mask in 10 minutes or less amidst the scarcity of face masks, which, most importantly, are reserved for healthcare professionals. Not only that, but I have also ensured that the fabrics recommended are capable of reducing the spread of the coronavirus when worn. The step by step process of making homemade face masks has also been simplified to make it easy for you to understand and follow through with. Lastly, I have shared many important tips you need in practicing safe wearing and removal of face masks, which is all but essential toward preventing yourself from the infections of viruses and toxic particles that your mask may harbor without your knowledge. Therefore, it is my sincere desire that you found great value from the invaluable and simplified insights shared in this book, which I hope you put into action right away.

Given the current global pandemic, I urge you to take full responsibility for your overall health and wellbeing.

I wish you the very best.

# References

Seladi-Schulman, J., PhD. (2020, April 6). Can Face Masks Protect You from the 2019 Coronavirus? What Types, When and How to Use. Retrieved from https://www.healthline.com/health/coronavirus-mask#protection

Lexie Sachs, Good Housekeeping Institute. (2020, April 13). How to Make Face Masks for Yourself and Hospitals During the Coronavirus Shortage. Retrieved from https://www.goodhousekeeping.com/health/a31902442/how-to-make-medical-face-masks/

Coronavirus Disease 2019 (COVID-19). (2020, February 11). Retrieved from https://www.cdc.gov/coronavirus/2019-ncov/prevent-getting-sick/diy-cloth-face-coverings.html

Instructables. (2020, April 19). DIY Cloth Face Mask. Retrieved from https://www.instructables.com/id/DIY-Cloth-Face-Mask/

Sampol, C. (2020, April 15). Surgical Masks, Respirators, Barrier Masks: Which Masks Actually Protect Against Coronavirus? Retrieved from http://emag.medicalexpo.com/which-masks-actually-protect-against-coronavirus/

Barking Up The Wrong Tree - How to be awesome at life. (n.d.). Retrieved December 10, 2019, from https://www.bakadesuyo.com

Influenza Virus Aerosols in Human Exhaled Breath: Particle Size, Culturability, and Effect of Surgical Masks. (2013, March 1). Retrieved from https://www.ncbi.nlm.nih.gov/pmc/articles/PMC3591312/

Meagan Visser. (2020, March 14). Homemade Essential Oil Hand Sanitizer Recipes For Adults & Children. Retrieved from https://www.growingupherbal.com/homemade-essential-oil-hand-sanitizer/

Leiva, C. (2020, April 8). The Best Materials For DIY Face Masks And Filters. Retrieved from https://www.huffpost.com/entry/best-materials-diy-face-masks-filters_l_5e8ce4c6c5b6e1a2e0fb4ada

Holland, K. (2019, April 18). Mercury Detox: Separating Fact from Fiction. Retrieved from https://www.healthline.com/health/mercury-detox#reducing-exposure

How to Make a No-Sew Face Mask in Less Than 5 Minutes. (2020, April 10). Retrieved from https://www.thespruce.com/no-sew-mask-4801991

www.ingramcontent.com/pod-product-compliance
Lightning Source LLC
Chambersburg PA
CBHW052101110526
44591CB00013B/2298